The Landlord's Emergency Manual for Filing an Insurance Claim

By Sam Shorrosh, Ph.D. – Catastrophe Adjuster

Published by Aspire Words 2024

COPYRIGHT NOTICE

Copyright © 2024 by AspireWords.com at https://aspirewords.com. All Rights Reserved.

The content, organization, gathering, compilation, magnetic translation, digital conversion and other matters related to this eBook are protected under applicable copyrights, trademarks, and other proprietary (including but not limited to intellectual property) rights, and, the copying, redistribution, selling, or publication by anyone of any such content or any part of the eBook is prohibited.

This eBook is for your own personal, non-transferrable, informational use only as per your agreement to our website's Terms and Conditions. The copying, distribution, publication, and reproduction of this eBook without permission is a theft of the author's intellectual property.

You must seek permission from the author to use content from this eBook except for brief quotations you can use as part of your book review but in those cases, you must still give proper credit to the author of this eBook.

If you would like permission to use content from this eBook for any other purpose, please contact us at sashorrosh52159@aspirewords.com.

DISCLAIMER

This eBook is presented to you for informational purposes only and is not a substitute for any kind of professional, legal, medical/health, finance, real estate, investing, adjusting advice. The content of this eBook is based solely on the personal views and opinions of the author, should not be considered scientific or correct conclusions, and do not represent the views of others.

All information provided in this eBook is "as is" and without warranty of any kind, expressed or implied.

Although we strive to provide accurate general information in this eBook, we do not guarantee that the content is free from any errors or omissions, and you should not rely solely on this information. Always consult a professional in the area for your specific needs and circumstances prior to making any professional, business, legal, and financial or tax-related decisions.

The author of this eBook is not engaged in the practice of rendering any professional advice. You agree that under no circumstances, the author and/or our officers, employees, successors, shareholders, joint venture partners or anyone else working with the author shall be liable for any direct, indirect, incidental, consequential, equitable, special, punitive, exemplary or any other damages resulting from your use of this eBook including but not limited to all the content, information, stories and products presented here.

We may share success stories of other people in this eBook as examples to motivate you, but it does not serve as a guarantee or promise of any kind for your results and successes if you decide to use the same information and insurance policy or adjusting type tips offered here. It is your sole responsibility to independently review the content of this eBook and any decisions you make, and the consequences thereof are your own.

We reserve the right to update the content and information in this eBook from time to time as needed. This eBook may contain affiliate links, which means we may earn a small commission if you purchase through our links at no extra cost to you.

We only provide these affiliate products for your convenience, but we have no control over these external websites, and they are solely responsible for their own content and information presented. We recommend these based on our individual experiences, but you are solely responsible for conducting your own due diligence to ensure you have obtained complete accurate information about these affiliate products. See the full disclaimer policy on our website.

Contents

COPYRIGHT NOTICE 3

DISCLAIMER 4

Introduction 10

Chapter 1: Understanding Your Insurance Policy 14

    Overview of Property Insurance Policies 14

    Types of Coverage...14

    Decoding Key Terms and Definitions in Property Insurance Policies .19

    Identifying Specific Peril Coverage 21

    The Importance of Endorsements and Riders...................................22

    Conclusion..23

Chapter 2: Preparing for a Claim Before Damage Occurs 29

    2.1 Conducting a Risk Assessment..29

    2.2 Keeping Accurate Records...29

    2.3 Regularly Reviewing and Updating Your Policy 30

Chapter 3: Documenting Damage and Losses 35

    3.1 Initial Steps Post-Damage...35

    3.2 Gathering Evidence 39

    Photographing and Videotaping Affected Areas...............................39

    3.3 Detailed Damage Reports – Here are insights into what your adjuster will be doing behind the scenes..43

Chapter 4: Navigating the Claims Process 55

Step 1: Gather Necessary Information 55

Step 2: Review the Claim Form 56

Step 3: Complete the Basic Information 56

Step 4: Describe the Incident 56

Step 5: Detail the Damages 57

Step 6: Estimate Repair or Replacement Costs 57

Step 7: Loss of Use 58

Step 8: Sign and Date the Form... 58

Step 9: Submit the Claim Form 58

Step 10: Follow Up 59

Additional Tips.. 59

4.2 Communicating with Your Insurer 59

Strategies for Maintaining Clear and Concise Records 60

Importance of Follow-Up 61

Handling Requests for Additional Information or Documentation 62

4.3 Claim Investigation and Adjuster Visits........................ 63

Chapter 5: Working with Insurance Adjusters 67

5.1 Understanding the Role of the Adjuster 67

5.2 Building a Positive Working Relationship 70

5.3 Negotiating Settlements 73

Chapter 6: Common Pitfalls and How to Avoid Them 77

6.1 Underinsurance and Coverage Gaps 77

6.2 Miscommunication and Misunderstandings 78

6.3 Delay and Denial Tactics 79

6.1 Underinsurance and Coverage Gaps 81

6.2 Miscommunication and Misunderstandings 82

6.3 Delay and Denial Tactics 82

Chapter 7: Dealing with Claim Denials and Disputes 85

7.1 Understanding Claim Denials 85

7.2 Filing an Appeal 86

7.3 Seeking Legal Assistance 88

Chapter 8: Maximizing Your Claim Settlement 90

8.1 Accurate and Detailed Documentation 90

8.2 Utilizing Expert Opinions 91

8.3 Strategic Negotiation Tactics 93

Chapter 9: The Role of Public Adjusters 97

9.1 Who are Public Adjusters? 97

Chapter 10: Protecting Your Investment Property Post-Claim 114

10.1 Repair and Restoration Best Practices 114

10.2 Updating Your Insurance Policy 115

10.3 Implementing Long-Term Risk Management 117

Reference Section 119

Additional Resources Available from Sam Shorrosh and sold on Amazon 124

Final Thoughts 125

Introduction

Investment properties can be lucrative assets, but they also come with risks that can impact your financial stability. Natural disasters, vandalism, and other unforeseen events can cause considerable damage to your property. Understanding how to effectively file an insurance claim is crucial for protecting your investment.

"Filing an Investment Property Insurance Claim: What You Can't Not Know to Benefit from Your Policy," provides comprehensive guidance on navigating the complexities of property insurance claims, ensuring you can maximize your benefits and recover promptly from any setbacks.

Real Life Scenario: Following back-to-back hurricanes that hit Louisiana in 2020, I spoke with an investor whose family's income depended on the rental income from fifty rental houses. Out of these, forty-eight houses were so severely damaged that the tenants could not return. Contractors advised them it would take six to nine months to get them all repaired due to the shortage of subcontractors and materials after the storms.

This situation created an immense amount of stress and fear of financial ruin. Here are the numbers:

9 months of lost rent X $1200 per house (average) x 48 houses = $518,400.00.

Policy paid 80% of the lost rent: $518,400 X 80% = $414,720.00.

Deductibles ranged from 2% to 5% and averaged out to $4,200/house X 48 houses - $201,600.00.

As the family burned through their savings and cash reserves, trying to cover both the deductibles and the loss of rental income, it did not occur to them that their policy might help them recoup their losses.

However, their agent, hearing their plight and knowing they had filed forty-eight claims, contacted their insurance adjuster.

Working with the family and their accountant, the adjuster oversaw and directed their claim process. As a former accountant, the adjuster advised them to discuss several suggestions with their CPA. So, they used the loss of income check to cover the deductibles, leaving $213,120.00 ($4,440 X 48 houses) to catch up on every mortgage in arears.

Even though the deductibles were paid for by insurance proceeds, they still qualified as losses and were therefore deductible on their taxes, along with the 20% of lost rental income not covered by their policy.

At the suggestion of the adjuster, the investment property owner met with his CPA to prepare financial applications for the Small Business Administration loan guarantee program.

The low rates helped them refinance an average rate of 8% down to 3%, reducing their monthly expenses.

The investor was then able to advertise his rental homes as "Newly Renovated" and at higher rates than prior to the storm. An ongoing shortage of rentable homes in the area meant he had a waiting list, even at the higher prices.

He gained these advantages:
- Lower mortgage payments
- Lower interest rates on the mortgages
- Reductions in payoff times for a few of the homes.
- Instant increases in equity valuations by up to 30% thanks to the new appraised values on his properties
- Renovated properties, paid for from his lost income reimbursements.
- Huge tax deductions against income.
- Resulting in a windfall year.

It pays to know what your policy can do for you, how to properly prepare for disasters, develop a plan of attack to put into effect at a moment's notice.

It pays to know how to document your losses, who to call first after a loss, and much more.

My hope is to provide insight into how your policy can pay for your losses by sharing the things you can't not know about your insurance policy coverages.

I have helped hundreds of investment property owners, both residential, multifamily, and commercial apartment owners, get the maximum benefits out of their policies, without giving away their money to fee-based representatives.

My hope is you will find more than just one or two diamonds, and my hope is that you prosper in your goals to provide a legacy of provision for you and your families.

Sincerely,

Sam Shorrosh, Ph.D. – Senior Catastrophe Adjuster, Litigation Claims Specialist, Author, and after you read this book, your new best friend. Enjoy!

Chapter 1: Understanding Your Insurance Policy

Overview of Property Insurance Policies

Investment property insurance policies vary significantly in terms of coverage, exclusions, and limitations.

Understanding the types of coverage—basic, broad, and special—is essential for ensuring you have adequate protection.

Basic policies cover a limited number of perils, while broad policies offer more comprehensive coverage, and special policies provide the most extensive protection.

Each policy will have exclusions and limitations that you need to be aware of to avoid unexpected surprises during the claim process.

This section will also delve into policy declarations, which detail the coverage limits and deductibles applicable to your investment property.

Types of Coverage

Basic Form Coverage (DP-1)

Basic form coverage, also known as DP-1, offers the most fundamental level of protection. It covers named perils, meaning only specific risks explicitly listed in the policy are covered. These typically include:

- Fire and Lightning

- Windstorm and Hail
- Explosion
- Riot or Civil Commotion
- Aircraft
- Vehicles
- Smoke
- Vandalism and Malicious Mischief
- Volcanic Eruption

Pros:

- Lower premiums compared to other forms of coverage.
- Simple and straightforward, covering common perils.

Cons:

- Limited scope of coverage; many risks are not included.
- Actual Cash Value (ACV) basis, which factors in depreciation, potentially leading to lower payouts.

Broad Form Coverage (DP-2)

Broad form coverage, or DP-2, builds on the basic form by covering all perils included in DP-1, plus additional named perils. This form offers a more comprehensive scope of protection, typically including:

- All DP-1 Perils

- Burglary Damage
- Falling Objects
- Weight of Ice, Snow, or Sleet
- Accidental Discharge or Overflow of Water or Steam
- Freezing of Plumbing, Heating, Air Conditioning, or Automatic Fire Protective Sprinkler System
- Sudden and Accidental Damage from Artificially Generated Electrical Current
- Tearing Apart, Cracking, Burning, or Bulging of a Steam or Hot Water Heating System or an Appliance for Heating Water

Pros:

- Broader coverage with more perils included.
- Offers a better balance of protection and cost.

Cons:

- Still limited to named perils. If it is not listed, it is not covered.
- Often more expensive than basic coverage.

Special Form Coverage (DP-3)

Special form coverage, or DP-3, offers the most comprehensive protection available. It covers all risks of physical loss except those specifically excluded in the policy. This is often referred to as "all-risk" or "open peril" coverage.

Pros:

- Extensive protection, covering all types of loss unless specifically excluded.
- Typically provides replacement cost coverage, ensuring the property is restored to its original condition without depreciation.

Cons:

- Higher premiums due to the extensive coverage.
- Exclusions must be carefully reviewed; common exclusions may include wear and tear, intentional damage, and specific natural disasters like floods and earthquakes.

Additional Coverage Options

Regardless of the type of form chosen, landlords can often enhance their policies with additional coverage options such as:

- Liability Coverage: Protects against legal claims for injuries or damage that occur to the property.
- Loss of Rental Income: Reimburses lost rental income if the property becomes uninhabitable due to a covered loss.
- Building Code Upgrades: Covers the cost of bringing the property up to current building codes after a covered loss.

- Flood and Earthquake Insurance: Separate policies or endorsements to cover these specific perils, which are typically excluded from standard policies.

Conclusion

Choosing the right landlord property insurance coverage involves balancing cost with the level of protection needed.

Basic form coverage (DP-1) is cost-effective for those seeking fundamental protection.

Broad form coverage (DP-2) offers a middle ground with more covered perils.

Special form coverage (DP-3) provides the most comprehensive protection.

Landlords should carefully assess their risks and consult with insurance professionals to tailor their policies to their specific needs, ensuring robust protection against potential losses.

1.2 Reading and Interpreting Policy Language

Insurance policies are filled with legal jargon and complex terms that can be challenging to understand.

This section will help you decode the key terms and definitions commonly found in property insurance policies. We will explore how to identify specific peril coverage and the importance of endorsements and riders that can extend or modify your coverage.

By understanding the policy language, you will be better equipped to know what is and is not covered, helping you make informed decisions when filing a claim.

Decoding Key Terms and Definitions in Property Insurance Policies

Key Terms and Definitions

- Peril

    A peril is a specific risk or cause of loss covered by the insurance policy. Common perils include fire, theft, and windstorms.

    Identifying which perils are covered is crucial, as policies may vary significantly in the scope of protection they offer.

- Named Perils vs. All-Risk (Open Peril) Policies

    Named perils policies cover only the risks explicitly listed in the policy. *If a peril is not named, it is not covered.*

    All-risk or open peril policies, on the other hand, cover all risks of physical loss except those specifically excluded.

    This broader coverage type provides more extensive protection but is often more expensive.

- Actual Cash Value (ACV)

    ACV refers to the replacement cost of damaged or destroyed property minus depreciation.

    This means the insurer will pay out the current value of the item, considering its age and condition at the time of loss.

- Replacement Cost Value (RCV)

    RCV is the cost to replace the damaged property with new property of similar kind and quality, without deducting for depreciation.

    This type of coverage ensures that policyholders can fully restore their property to its original condition.

- Deductible

    The deductible is the amount the policyholder must pay out of pocket before the insurance coverage kicks in.

    Higher deductibles lower the premium but increase the initial cost burden during a claim.

- Exclusion

    Exclusions are specific conditions or circumstances for which the policy does not provide coverage.

    Common exclusions include damage due to war, nuclear hazards, and intentional acts by the insured.

- Endorsement

An endorsement, also known as a rider, is an amendment to the standard insurance policy that can add, remove, or modify coverage.

Endorsements allow policyholders to customize their insurance to better meet their specific needs.

Identifying Specific Peril Coverage

Understanding which perils are covered by your policy is fundamental to ensuring adequate protection. Here are some steps to identify specific peril coverage:

1. Review the Policy Declarations Page

- The declarations page provides an overview of the key components of your policy, including covered perils, coverage limits, and deductibles.

This page serves as a summary and a starting point for understanding your coverage.

2. Examine the Coverage Sections

- Policies typically have distinct sections for diverse types of coverage, such as dwelling, personal property, and liability.

Each section will outline the specific perils covered.

3. Read the Exclusions

- Carefully review the exclusions section to understand what is not covered.

This can help identify gaps in coverage that might need to be addressed with additional endorsements or separate policies.

4. Consult with Your Insurance Agent

- If there is any ambiguity or uncertainty about what perils are covered, discussing your policy with an insurance agent can provide clarity and ensure you have the right protection.

The Importance of Endorsements and Riders

Endorsements and riders play a crucial role in customizing insurance policies to better suit the unique needs of property owners. Here is why they are important:

1. Enhancing Coverage

- Standard policies often have limitations and exclusions that might leave significant risks uncovered.

Endorsements can extend coverage to include perils such as mechanical equipment failure, sewer backup, earthquake, or flood, which are typically excluded from standard policies.

2. Filling Coverage Gaps

- Property owners with unique or high-value items might need additional protection beyond the standard coverage limits.

Endorsements can be added to insure valuable individual property like jewelry, art, or antiques beyond the basic coverage.

3. Updating Coverage

- Over time, the needs of property owners can change. Endorsements allow for updates to the policy without the need to purchase a new one.

This can include increasing coverage limits, adding new insured locations, or adjusting deductible amounts.

4. Cost Management

- By selectively adding endorsements, property owners can tailor their coverage to address specific risks while managing their overall insurance costs.

This approach allows for a balance between comprehensive protection and affordability.

Conclusion

Decoding the terminology in property insurance policies is essential for understanding the coverage you have and identifying any potential gaps.

Recognizing key terms such as perils, ACV (Actual Cash Value), RCV (Replacement Cost Value), and exclusions can help clarify the scope of your policy.

Furthermore, endorsements and riders offer valuable tools to extend or modify coverage, ensuring your policy meets your specific needs.

By thoroughly reviewing your policy, consulting with your insurance agent, and making use of endorsements, you can secure comprehensive protection for your property investments.

1.3 Knowing Your Rights and Responsibilities

Landlord Policyholder's Rights and Responsibilities

As a landlord with property insurance, it is crucial to understand both your rights and responsibilities to ensure smooth and effective management of your insurance policy.

Knowing what is expected of you and what you can expect from your insurer can help in maintaining your property, managing claims, and ensuring that you receive the benefits of your coverage.

Maintaining the Property

One of the primary responsibilities of a landlord is to maintain the insured property in good condition.

Regular maintenance not only helps in preventing damage but also demonstrates to your insurer that you are taking proactive steps to mitigate risks.

This includes routine inspections, addressing repair needs promptly, and ensuring that safety measures such as smoke detectors and fire extinguishers are in place and functioning.

Proper maintenance can prevent minor issues from becoming major problems that could lead to claims.

Reporting Claims Promptly

Timely reporting of claims is another critical responsibility. If your property suffers damage or if an incident occurs that could lead to a claim, it is essential to notify your insurer as soon as possible.

Prompt reporting helps in the efficient processing of claims and ensures that the insurer can investigate the incident while evidence is fresh.

Delayed reporting can result in complications, such as difficulties in verifying the cause and extent of the damage, which could affect your claim settlement.

Cooperation During Claims Process

As a policyholder, you are required to cooperate fully with your insurer during the claims process.

This includes providing accurate and complete information about the incident, allowing the insurer to inspect the damaged property, and submitting any required documentation in a timely manner.

Cooperation helps in expediting the claims process and facilitates a fair and prompt settlement.

Duties of the Insurer

While landlords have specific responsibilities, insurers also have obligations they must fulfill.

Understanding these duties can help you hold your insurer accountable and ensure that your claims are managed properly.

Investigating Claims

One of the primary duties of an insurer is to investigate claims thoroughly and in good faith.

When a claim is filed, the insurer is responsible for assessing the damage, determining the cause, and verifying that the loss is covered under the policy.

This investigation should be conducted promptly and professionally.

The insurer may send an adjuster to inspect the property, interview witnesses, and gather necessary documentation to evaluate the claim.

But remember, proving the damages are related to a peril covered by the policy is your responsibility.

Settling Claims Fairly

Insurers are obligated to settle claims fairly and in accordance with the terms of the policy. This means providing compensation that accurately reflects the covered losses, without unjust delays or denials.

Fair settlement practices include clear communication with the policyholder, providing explanations for any coverage decisions, and paying out the claim amount promptly once the settlement is agreed upon.

Insurers must also act in good faith and not engage in practices that would unjustly delay or reduce the settlement.

Providing Policy Information and Updates

Insurers have a duty to keep policyholders informed about their coverage and any changes that may affect their policy.

This includes providing copies of the policy documents, issuing renewal notices, and communicating any changes in terms or premiums.

Additionally, insurers should be available to answer questions and provide guidance on policy coverage and claims procedures.

Conclusion

Understanding the rights and responsibilities of both landlord policyholders and insurers is essential for managing property insurance effectively.

As a landlord, maintaining your property and reporting claims promptly are key responsibilities that help in mitigating risks and ensuring smooth claims processing.

On the other hand, insurers are obligated to investigate claims thoroughly, settle them fairly, and keep policyholders informed about their coverage.

By knowing what is expected from each party, landlords can navigate the insurance process more confidently and ensure they receive the full benefits of their policy.

Chapter 2: Preparing for a Claim Before Damage Occurs

2.1 Conducting a Risk Assessment

Before any damage occurs, it is important to conduct a thorough risk assessment of your investment property.

This involves identifying potential risks and vulnerabilities, such as the property's location in a flood zone or its susceptibility to vandalism.

By understanding these risks, you can implement preventive measures, such as installing security systems or reinforcing structures, to mitigate potential damage.

2.2 Keeping Accurate Records

Maintaining accurate records of your property assets is crucial for supporting your insurance claims.

This section will guide you on how to keep an up-to-date inventory of all items within the property, including furniture, appliances, and fixtures.

We will also cover the importance of photographing and documenting the condition of the property regularly to provide a clear record of its pre-damage state.

2.3 Regularly Reviewing and Updating Your Policy

Maintaining adequate insurance coverage is crucial for landlords to protect their investment properties.

Regular reviews and updates to your insurance policy ensure that your coverage keeps pace with any changes in the property and its value.

Here are some key strategies for effectively managing and updating your landlord insurance policy.

Conduct Regular Property Assessments

Regular property assessments help in understanding the current state and value of your investment.

Conduct thorough inspections at least annually to identify any significant changes or improvements.

Renovations, new appliances, or upgraded systems can increase the property's value, requiring adjustments to your policy limits to ensure adequate coverage.

Additionally, assessments help in spotting any new risks that need to be covered.

Review Policy Limits and Coverage Types

1. Assess Property Value Changes:

    The market value of your property can fluctuate due to numerous factors such as local real estate trends, renovations, or changes in the neighborhood.

Regularly appraising your property helps you determine whether the coverage limits need to be increased or decreased to reflect its true value.

2. Evaluate Coverage Types:

As your property changes, so should your insurance coverage.

Evaluate whether your current policy types still meet your requirements.

For instance, if you add a new rental unit, you may need additional liability coverage or a separate policy for the new unit.

3. Update Replacement Cost Estimates:

Replacement cost values can change over time due to inflation and rising costs of materials and labor.

Ensure that your policy's replacement cost coverage is updated to reflect these changes, so you are fully covered in the event of a total loss.

Add or Adjust Endorsements and Riders

Endorsements and riders allow you to customize your policy to better meet your specific needs. Here is how you can effectively manage these:

1. Add New Endorsements:

If your property now includes additional structures like a shed or a garage, or if you have installed high-value systems such as solar panels, consider adding endorsements to cover these additions.

2. Adjust Existing Riders:

Reassess existing riders periodically. For example, if you previously had an endorsement for a swimming pool that you have since removed, you can eliminate that rider to reduce your premium.

Conversely, if you have added new features or assets, update your riders accordingly.

3. Consider Liability Limits:

Increasing the liability limits on your policy might be necessary if your property's usage has changed, such as an increase in the number of tenants or additional public access areas.

Higher liability limits offer better protection against potential lawsuits.

Stay Informed About Policy Changes

Insurance companies periodically update their policies and terms. Staying informed about these changes can help you make necessary adjustments to your coverage:

1. Regularly Communicate with Your Insurance Agent:

Schedule regular meetings with your insurance agent to review your policy. They can provide insights into new coverage options, changes in insurance laws, and recommend adjustments based on your current situation.

2. Review Policy Documents:

Carefully read any policy updates or renewal documents sent by your insurer. Look for changes in terms, conditions, and coverage limits that could affect your protection.

3. Ask for a Policy Audit:

Request a professional audit of your policy from your insurance company or an independent consultant. This can provide an objective evaluation of your coverage and identify any gaps or areas for improvement.

Adjusting for Changes in Tenancy

Changes in tenancy can also affect your insurance needs:

1. Short-Term vs. Long-Term Rentals:

If you switch from long-term leases to short-term vacation rentals, your insurance needs may change. Short-term rentals often require additional liability coverage and may involve higher risks.

2. Tenant Improvements:

If tenants make significant improvements or modifications to the property, these should be reported to your insurer. Such changes might increase the property's value and risk profile, necessitating adjustments to your coverage.

3. Occupancy Rates:

Fluctuations in occupancy rates can impact your insurance needs. For instance, vacant properties might require vacancy coverage due to the increased risk of vandalism or undetected damage.

Conclusion

Regularly reviewing and updating your landlord insurance policy is essential to ensure that your coverage remains adequate and relevant.

By conducting regular property assessments, reviewing, and adjusting policy limits and coverage types, adding, or adjusting endorsements and riders, staying informed about policy changes, and considering changes in tenancy, landlords can protect their investments effectively.

Working closely with your insurance agent and staying proactive in managing your policy can provide peace of mind and financial security.

Chapter 3: Documenting Damage and Losses

3.1 Initial Steps Post-Damage

When damage occurs, the first steps you take can significantly impact your insurance claim.

This section provides a detailed guide on ensuring safety and mitigating further damage immediately after an incident. It covers the importance of contacting your insurance company promptly to report the damage and begin the claims process.

Initial Steps Post-Damage

When your investment property sustains damage, taking immediate and appropriate action is crucial to ensure a smooth claims process and minimize further losses.

Here are the essential steps you should follow right after discovering damage to your property:

1. **Ensure Safety First**

    The priority after discovering damage is to ensure the safety of your tenants and their families.

    If the damage has created a hazardous environment, such as structural instability, electrical hazards, or gas leaks, they should evacuate the property immediately.

    Call emergency services if necessary to address any urgent threats to health and safety.

2. Document the Damage

Thorough documentation of the damage is essential for a successful insurance claim. Follow these steps to ensure you capture all necessary details:

- Photographs and Videos: Take clear, detailed photographs and videos of all visible damage. Include multiple angles and close-up shots to capture the extent of the damage. Document both the exterior and interior of the property.

- Written Descriptions: Write detailed descriptions of the damage, noting the specific areas affected and the apparent cause. Be as precise as possible, including measurements if relevant.

- Inventory of Damaged Items: Create an inventory list of all damaged individual property, fixtures, and structural elements. Note the condition of each item, the estimated value, and any relevant receipts or proof of purchase if available.

3. Mitigate Further Damage

To prevent additional damage and protect your property, take immediate steps to mitigate the impact of the initial damage.

Here are some key actions you can take:

- Temporary Repairs: Make temporary repairs to secure the property and prevent further damage. This might include tarping a damaged roof, boarding up broken windows, or shutting off water to prevent flooding. Keep receipts for any materials or services used for these repairs, as they may be reimbursable under your insurance policy.

- Water Extraction: If the property has suffered water damage, begin the process of water extraction and drying as soon as possible to prevent mold growth and further structural damage. Consider hiring a professional water damage restoration service if the damage is extensive.

4. Notify Your Insurance Company

Promptly notifying your insurance company is critical for initiating the claims process. Follow these steps to ensure a smooth notification:

- Contact Information: Have your insurance policy number and the contact information for your insurance agent readily available.

- Report the Damage: Call your insurance company's claims department or your insurance agent to report the damage. Provide them with a detailed account of what happened, the extent of the damage, and any immediate actions you have taken to mitigate further damage.

- Follow Instructions: Follow the instructions provided by your insurer regarding next steps, which may include scheduling an inspection by an insurance adjuster and submitting your documentation.

5. Keep a Claims Journal

Maintaining a detailed claims journal can help you stay organized and track the progress of your claim. Your claims journal should include:

- Chronological Log: Keep a chronological log of all communications with your insurance company, including dates, times, and names of representatives you spoke with.

- Documentation of Actions Taken: Record all actions taken to mitigate damage, including receipts for temporary repairs and any correspondence with contractors or emergency services.

- Inspection and Repair Notes: Document the dates and details of any inspections conducted by insurance adjusters or contractors, as well as estimates and invoices for repair work.

Conclusion

Taking these initial steps post-damage is crucial for ensuring the safety of occupants, protecting your property from further harm, and setting the stage for a successful insurance claim.

By promptly documenting the damage, mitigating further risks, and communicating effectively with your insurance company, you can navigate the aftermath of property damage with confidence and efficiency.

3.2 Gathering Evidence

Effective documentation is key to a successful insurance claim.

This section outlines how to gather evidence of damage, including photographing and videotaping the affected areas. We will discuss the types of evidence that are most compelling and how to organize and present this information to your insurer.

Photographing and Videotaping Affected Areas

1. Preparing to Document:
- Before you begin, ensure you have a decent quality camera or smartphone with sufficient storage and battery life. Having a notebook or digital device to take notes can also be beneficial.

2. Photographs:
- Overview Shots: Start with wide-angle shots of the entire affected area to provide context. Capture the front, back, and sides of the property, and any relevant surrounding areas.

- Detailed Shots: Take close-up photos of specific damage. Focus on structural elements like walls, roofs, floors, and foundations. Highlight any visible cracks, water stains, broken windows, or other defects.

- Damaged Items: Photograph any private property, appliances, or fixtures that were damaged. Include serial numbers, make, and model information where applicable.

- Different Angles: Shoot from multiple angles to ensure that the damage is fully visible. This includes both horizontal and vertical shots.

- Before and After: If possible, provide photos from before the damage occurred for comparison. This can be particularly useful if you have recent images of the property in good condition.

3. *Videotaping:*

- Walkthrough Videos: Conduct a video walkthrough of the entire property. Narrate as you go, describing the damage and pointing out specific areas of concern. This can provide a more comprehensive view than photos alone.

- Focus on Details: Zoom in on specific areas of damage and describe what you are seeing. For example, if there is water damage, mention the color, size, and location of the stains.

- Real-Time Commentary: Offer real-time commentary to explain the extent and impact of the damage. Highlight any potential safety hazards or areas that need urgent attention.

Types of Evidence That Are Most Compelling

1. *Time-Stamped Media:*
   - Ensure that all photos and videos are time-stamped. This verifies when the evidence was collected and can support your timeline of events.

2. *Comparative Evidence:*
   - Before-and-after photos are highly compelling as they clearly show the impact of the damage. This comparison can effectively demonstrate the extent of the loss.

3. *Written Descriptions and Notes:*
   - Detailed written descriptions accompany visual evidence. Note the specific type of damage, location, and potential cause. This contextual information can help the insurance adjuster understand the situation better.

4. *Professional Assessments:*
   - If possible, include assessments from professionals such as contractors, engineers, or home inspectors. Their expert opinions on the damage can add credibility to your claim.

5. *Receipts and Estimates:*
   - Gather receipts for any emergency repairs or temporary fixes you have undertaken. Also, obtain repair estimates from licensed contractors to provide a cost perspective on the damage.

Organizing and Presenting Information to the Insurer

1. Categorize the Evidence:
- Organize your evidence into categories such as structural damage, personal property damage, and temporary repairs. This makes it easier for the insurer to review.

2. Create a Comprehensive Report:
- Compile all evidence into a comprehensive report. Include an introduction that summarizes the incident, followed by sections that detail each category of damage. Attach photos and videos within the relevant sections, along with written descriptions.

3. Digital Presentation:
- Use digital tools to create a well-organized presentation. Consider creating a PDF document or a digital folder with labeled subfolders for each type of evidence. This can streamline the review process for your insurer.

4. Clear and Concise Documentation:
- Ensure that all documentation is clear and concise. Avoid jargon and stick to factual descriptions.
- Highlight key pieces of evidence and make sure each item is easy to locate within your report.

5. Submit and Follow Up:
    - Submit your evidence through the preferred method of your insurer, whether it is via an online portal, email, or physical copies.

    - Follow up with your insurance adjuster to confirm receipt and address any questions they may have. Never assume that what you mailed or emailed arrived.

Conclusion

Gathering and organizing evidence of property damage is a meticulous process that pays off eventually. By following these steps, you ensure that your claim is well-supported, and that the insurance adjuster has all the information needed to assess your situation accurately.

Detailed documentation, clear presentation, and professional assessments can significantly enhance the credibility of your claim and expedite the resolution process.

3.3 Detailed Damage Reports – Here are insights into what your adjuster will be doing behind the scenes.

Writing comprehensive damage reports is essential for a smooth claims process.

This section provides tips on how you can help your adjuster by describing the damage in detail, including the extent of the damage and the estimated cost of repairs.

We will also cover how to include contractor assessments and estimates to support your claim.

Structuring Your Damage Report

1. Introduction:

- **Summary of the Incident:** Begin with a summary of the incident that caused the damage. Include the date, time, and nature of the event (e.g., storm, fire, flood).

- **Property Information:** Provide essential details about the property, including the address, type of property (single-family home, multi-unit rental, etc.), and any relevant background information.

2. Overview of Damages:

- **General Description:** Offer a general overview of the damage. Highlight the most severely affected areas and give a sense of the overall extent of the damage.

- **Scope of the Report:** Clarify what the report will cover. Specify whether it includes only visible damage or also potential underlying issues that need further investigation.

Categorizing Damage

1. Structural Damage:
    - Exterior Damage: Document damage to the roof, siding, windows, doors, foundation, and any other external features. Include photographs with descriptions of each damaged area.
    - Interior Damage: Report damage to walls, ceilings, floors, and fixtures. Detail the extent of the damage, such as water stains, cracks, or structural shifts.

2. Personal Property Damage:
    - Inventory of Damaged Items: Create an itemized list of damaged personal property, including furniture, electronics, appliances, and other valuables you provide for use in the rental property.

      Differentiate anything that belongs to the tenant as they will file for their own losses under their rental policy.

      For each item of yours, note the make, model, age, quantity, and estimated value.

    - Supporting Documentation: Attach receipts, warranties, or appraisals that support the value of each item.

      Photographs of each item in its damaged state are also crucial.

Printouts from websites that show the same or similar items, descriptions and price are usually acceptable as forms of proof of loss.

3. Loss of Use:
    - Temporary Relocation Costs: If the property is uninhabitable, detail the costs associated with temporary relocation, such as hotel stays, rental expenses, and additional living costs.

        For example, if you own a duplex and live on one side, you may also have relocation costs due to your property being uninhabitable.

        Keep in mind, *your tenant is responsible for their own relocation costs.*

        One of the conditions of your rental contract should stipulate tenants must show proof of a rental policy that covers their contents, liability, costs to relocate and additional living expenses.

    - Lost Rental Income: For investment properties, include documentation of lost rental income due to tenant displacement.

        Provide copies of lease agreements and rent rolls as evidence.

        Know the specifics of how long the coverage will last, and what percentage of the rents will be reimbursed.

You will want to keep this information to file at tax time, as anything not covered should be applied as a loss against income.

Check with your accountant for what would apply and how much.

Supporting Evidence

1. Photographic Evidence:
   - Comprehensive Coverage: Ensure that photographs cover all aspects of the damage. Include both wide-angle shots for context and close-up shots for detail.
   - Annotated Photos: Annotate photos with descriptions and notes to clarify the specific damage shown. Use arrows or circles to highlight areas of concern.

2. Videos:
   - Narrated Walkthroughs: Create video walkthroughs of the property, narrating as you go to explain the damage. This helps provide a more dynamic and comprehensive view than photos alone.

     Make it a pattern that every time the property is vacated, and you do necessary upkeep and maintenance, you take a video and photos of the condition of the property so that you have before the storm and after the storm documentation.
   - Focused Clips: Include short video clips focusing on significant damage areas, providing a detailed look at specific issues.

Always begin at the entrance and move around the room in a slow circle, putting the damage into the context of the overall space, and then zooming in for closeups of specific areas.

3. Professional Assessments:
   - Contractor Estimates: Attach estimates from licensed contractors for the repair work.

   These should detail the scope of work, materials needed, labor costs, and timelines.

   Note that your insurer will insist on inspecting the property BEFORE any significant repairs are done.

   They will stipulate that only temporary repairs are permitted prior to their inspection, and if any plumbing is involved you must hang onto the damaged parts that are removed to perform repairs.

   Estimates from water mitigation contractors are often a problem due to poorly written descriptions of the damage, repairs initiated, and may lack photo support. Ask for this information.

   BE ADVISED: Most policies allow only up to $3,000 to perform emergency or initial mitigation.

   The mitigation company MUST provide an estimate for review and approval, before they break that threshold, or their invoice could be rejected, leaving you to fight it out with the mitigation company.

Do not be manipulated by the contractors trying to get forgiveness rather than permission.

- Engineering Reports: If applicable, include reports from structural engineers or other specialists who have assessed the damage and provided professional opinions.

  If your insurer hires an engineer to inspect your property, ask for a copy of the report.

  You have the right to see what they report as it may be the key element that determines whether your insurer provides you coverage.

  If you disagree with the engineer's determination you have the right to hire your own engineer at your own expense to provide a rebuttal.

  Insider Recommendation: If the carrier accepts your engineer's report over their own engineer, or because they did not hire one, you should request they reimburse you for the cost of hiring your own engineer.

- Specialist Reports: If required, you have the right to hire an asbestos or lead paint specialist. Typically, if their report proves to be correct, and your insurer agrees with the expert's conclusions, they may reimburse you for the cost of the specialist's report.

  However, that can go both ways and if they reject the report may refuse to pay the experts' fee on your behalf.

So, be careful when a public adjuster pressures you to let him bring in a friend who does air quality testing, lead paint and asbestos or mold testing, without getting permission first from the carrier.

Your insurer may have their own people they use, or they may not believe the demand for those add-on services is warranted.

If you sign a contract either through the public adjuster or directly with his "pals," you could be on the hook for thousands of dollars in frivolous and unnecessary expenses.

Organization and Presentation

1. Clear and Logical Structure:

- Section Headers: Your adjuster's estimate will use clear headers and sub-headers to organize the report into distinct sections. This helps the reader quickly locate specific information. Consider using that same structure for your own records and reporting.

- Table of Contents: Your adjuster's report may include a table of contents at the beginning of the report for easy navigation. This is not as crucial when you have a small claim but in a large-loss or total-loss situation, it could really help you jump right to the parts you need to find quickly.

2. Detailed Descriptions:
   - Objective and Factual: Your adjuster must use descriptions that are objective and factual.

     He should avoid subjective language and stick to clear, concise explanations.

     Not everyone has a strong education background, so consider what you are reading and if you have questions, please ask your adjuster for clarification.

     In the same way, if you write up your own report to submit to the carrier, have a close friend or someone in your family, read your report aloud to see if it makes sense. Do not get upset, just think through what you are trying to communicate and why.

   - Measurements and Specifications: Where applicable, your adjuster is expected to include measurements, specifications, and other technical details that provide a thorough understanding of the damage.

   - Photos: Definitely, photos are worth thousands of dollars in establishing the scope and nature of damage. Make sure to look at the photos taken by your contractor, adjuster, or others as you may notice things others might have missed, or they could reveal that someone has overexaggerated or undervalued their estimate.

     For example, are the vents and drip edges painted? If they are, your policy pays to paint the replacement vents or drip edges. Be aware the contractor may put it in his estimate but then not paint, putting the cost difference in his own pocket. However, if you choose for them to not be repainted, that line item is money in your pocket, which you could apply toward your deductible.

3. Appendices:

- Supporting Documents: Use appendices to include additional supporting documents, such as receipts, invoices, content lists, contact information for where you will be while repairs are underway.

  Provide up to date information as to who is on your policy (death, divorce, estrangement, should lead to updating your data with your Agent), professional assessments, and legal documents like power of attorney letters, letters of representation showing that you hired a public adjuster or attorney (although these should be sent by those parties to the insurance company).

- Cross-Referencing: Cross-reference these documents within the main report to show how they support specific claims. You may have to up your game when it comes to writing everything down in a way that makes sense, so do not be afraid to ask for help.

3.3.5 Submission and Follow-Up

1. Submission:

   - Format: Submit the report in a format preferred by your insurer, whether it is a digital PDF, an online submission through a claim portal, or physical copies.

   - Confirmation: Obtain confirmation from your insurer that they have received the report and all supporting documents. If your files are too big, they may not go through.

     Rather than wait until the recipient figures out, they did not get the files you sent, call them, and confirm receipt. You may need to resend the file in smaller chunks.

     For example, I never email more than twenty pictures with one email. If your camera is hi-definition, expect to send even fewer photos. Typically, your catastrophe company can handle only about 5 MB per email.

2. Follow-Up:

   - Regular Updates: Stay in regular contact with your insurance adjuster, at least every two weeks. Provide any additional information they may request promptly and if you must relocate, let them know how to reach you.

   - Addressing Queries: Be prepared to answer questions or provide further evidence as needed. Your policy has verbiage that states answering questions and providing evidence are your responsibility and not doing so could result in your claim being rejected for breach of contractual obligation. Maintaining open communication can help expedite the claims process.

Conclusion

Creating detailed damage reports is a critical step in the property insurance claims process.

By systematically documenting and presenting evidence of the damage, you ensure that your claim is well supported, and that the insurer has all the necessary information to process it efficiently.

Clear organization, comprehensive evidence, and professional assessments are key components of a successful damage report.

Chapter 4: Navigating the Claims Process

4.1 Filing the Claim

Filing an insurance claim involves completing various forms and providing detailed information about the damage.

This section offers step-by-step instructions for filling out claim forms accurately and thoroughly.

We will also highlight common mistakes to avoid during this process to prevent delays or denials of your claim.

Step-by-Step Instructions for Filling Out Claim Forms Accurately and Thoroughly

Filing an insurance claim can be a daunting task, but by following these detailed steps, you can ensure your claim forms are filled out accurately and thoroughly, increasing the likelihood of a smooth and successful claims process.

Step 1: Gather Necessary Information

Before you start filling out your claim forms, gather all the necessary information and documents. This includes:

- Your insurance policy number.
- Detailed information about the property (address, type, etc.).
- Date and time of the incident causing the damage.
- A detailed description of the incident.

- Photos and videos of the damage.
- Receipts and records of damaged items.
- Any professional assessments or repair estimates.

Step 2: Review the Claim Form

Carefully review the entire claim form before you start filling it out. This will give you an idea of the required information and help you avoid missing any sections. If available, read the instructions or guidelines provided by your insurer.

Special Note: Educators tell us that people learn in multiple ways. They use descriptive terms like Auditory, Visual, Kinesthetic and Tactile. Bear in mind that people who learn differently than you will communicate differently as well.

Step 3: Complete the Basic Information

Begin with the basic information required on the form:

- Policyholder Information: Enter your full name, address, contact details, and your policy number.
- Property Details: Provide the address and type of the property (e.g., single-family home, multi-unit rental).

Step 4: Describe the Incident

In this section, you will describe the incident that caused the damage:

- Date and Time: Enter the exact date and time when the incident occurred.

- Type of Incident: Specify the type of incident (e.g., storm, fire, flood).

- Description of Incident: Provide a detailed account of what happened. Be clear, concise, and factual. Include any relevant circumstances leading to the damage.

Step 5: Detail the Damages

This is where you itemize the damages:

- List Damaged Areas/Items: Create a detailed list of all damaged areas and items. Include descriptions and the extent of the damage.

- Supporting Evidence: Attach or reference any photos, videos, receipts, or professional assessments. Ensure that each piece of evidence is clearly labeled and corresponds to the items listed.

Step 6: Estimate Repair or Replacement Costs

Provide an estimate for the cost of repairs or replacements:

- Repair Estimates: If you have obtained repair estimates from contractors, include these. Detail the costs of materials and labor.

- Replacement Costs: For items that need to be replaced, provide the estimated cost of purchasing new ones. Include receipts or proof of value for expensive items.

Step 7: Loss of Use

If applicable, document any additional living expenses or loss of rental income:

- **Temporary Accommodation Costs:** Include receipts for hotel stays, temporary rentals, and additional living expenses incurred due to the property being uninhabitable.

- **Loss of Rental Income:** Provide documentation of lost rental income, such as lease agreements and rent rolls.

Step 8: Sign and Date the Form

Once you have filled out all the required sections, carefully review the entire form to ensure accuracy and completeness. Sign and date the form where required. Your signature attests to the accuracy and truthfulness of the information provided.

Step 9: Submit the Claim Form

Submit the completed claim form along with all supporting documentation to your insurer:

- **Preferred Method:** Use the submission method preferred by your insurer, whether it is through an online portal, email, or postal mail.

- **Confirmation:** Obtain confirmation of receipt from your insurer. This can be a submission receipt from an online portal or a confirmation email.

Step 10: Follow Up

After submission, stay proactive in the follow-up process:

- **Regular Contact:** Maintain regular contact with your insurance adjuster to check on the status of your claim.
- **Additional Information:** Be prepared to provide any additional information or clarification that the insurer might request.

Additional Tips

- **Accuracy:** Double-check all information for accuracy. Errors or omissions can delay the processing of your claim.
- **Thorough Documentation:** Ensure all supporting documents are well-organized and clearly labeled.
- **Professional Help:** If the claim is complex, consider seeking help from a public adjuster or a professional experienced in filing insurance claims.

By following these steps meticulously, you can ensure that your claim forms are filled out accurately and thoroughly, helping to facilitate a smoother and more efficient claims process.

4.2 Communicating with Your Insurer

Effective communication with your insurer is crucial throughout the claims process.

This section provides strategies for maintaining clear and concise records of all communications with your insurance company.

We will also discuss the importance of follow-up and how to handle requests for additional information or documentation.

Strategies for Maintaining Clear and Concise Records

1. **Use Written Communication Whenever Possible:**
   - Whenever you communicate with your insurance company, especially for important matters, do so in writing (email or formal letters). This creates a documented trail that you can refer to if needed.
2. **Document Phone Calls:**
   - For phone calls, take detailed notes during the conversation. Record the date, time, names of the representatives you spoke with, and a summary of the discussion. Follow up the call with an email summarizing what was discussed and agreed upon.
3. **Organize Your Documentation:**
   - Create a dedicated folder (either physical or digital) to store all correspondence related to your insurance claim. Organize documents chronologically or by category (e.g., emails, letters, notes from phone calls).

4. Save Electronic Communications:
    - Save copies of all emails and digital communications with your insurer. Consider creating subfolders to categorize emails based on topics or dates.
5. Confirm Important Discussions in Writing:
    - If you have a significant conversation or reach an agreement over the phone, follow up immediately with an email summarizing the discussion and any agreements made. Request confirmation from the insurer to ensure mutual understanding.

Importance of Follow-Up

1. Stay Proactive:
    - Regularly follow up with your insurance company to check on the status of your claim. This demonstrates your commitment to resolving the issue and ensures that your claim remains a priority.
2. Timely Responses:
    - Respond promptly to any requests for additional information or documentation from your insurer. Delayed responses can prolong the claims process and may lead to unnecessary complications.
3. Keep a Record of Follow-Ups:
    - Document each follow-up communication, including the date, method of communication, and a summary of the discussion or outcome.

This helps track the progress of your claim and any outstanding actions.

Handling Requests for Additional Information or Documentation

1. Review the Request Carefully:
   - Carefully review any requests for additional information or documentation from your insurer. Understand what is being asked and why it is needed to process your claim.
2. Provide Complete and Accurate Information:
   - Ensure that you provide all requested information accurately and in a timely manner. Incomplete or inaccurate information can delay the processing of your claim.
3. Document Your Submission:
   - Keep a copy of all documents and information you submit to the insurer. Note the date of submission and any confirmation of receipt you receive.
4. Follow Up if Necessary:
   - If you do not receive confirmation of receipt or acknowledgment of the information provided within a reasonable time, follow up with your insurer to ensure they have received and processed your submission.

By implementing these strategies, you can maintain clear and concise records of all communications with your insurance company, stay proactive in following up on your claim, and effectively handle requests for additional information or documentation. This proactive approach not only facilitates a smoother claims process but also helps ensure that your rights as a policyholder are upheld.

4.3 Claim Investigation and Adjuster Visits

Once your claim is filed, an adjuster will visit your property to assess the damage.

This section explains what to expect during an adjuster's inspection and how to prepare for it.

We will provide tips on how to assist the adjuster and ensure that all damage is thoroughly documented and evaluated.

What to Expect During an Adjuster's Inspection

When an insurance adjuster visits your property to assess damage after filing a claim, it is essential to be prepared and understand the process. Here is what you can expect during an adjuster's inspection and how to make the most of the visit:

Scheduling the Inspection

Typically, your insurance company will contact you to schedule the adjuster's visit. It is important to confirm the appointment and make sure you or a representative will be present during the inspection. If possible, try to schedule the inspection at a time when you can dedicate your full attention to the process.

Documentation Preparation

Before the adjuster arrives, gather all relevant documentation related to the claim:

- Claim Details: Have a copy of your insurance policy and the claim documentation where you can easily access it. Do not just rely on your memory as it could cost you money.
- Evidence of Damage: Organize photographs, videos, and any other evidence you have collected to document the damage. Label them clearly and prepare to present them to the adjuster.
- Records and Estimates: If you have obtained repair estimates or assessments from contractors, have them available for review.

Walkthrough and Inspection Process

During the inspection, the adjuster will:

- Assess Damage: The adjuster will conduct a thorough inspection of the affected areas. Be prepared to provide access to all parts of the property where damage is claimed.
- Documentation Review: Present your evidence systematically. Explain the extent of the damage and how it aligns with your claim. Provide any supporting documents that validate your claim, such as receipts for repairs or replacements.

Communication and Cooperation

- **Answer Questions Honestly:** Be transparent and provide accurate information in response to the adjuster's questions. If you are unsure about something, it is okay to say so.
- **Take Notes:** Document the adjuster's observations and notes during the inspection. This can help clarify any discrepancies or misunderstandings later.

After the Inspection

After the inspection, ask the adjuster for a timeline on when you can expect to receive their assessment and report. Confirm any next steps or additional information required from your end. Follow up with your insurance company promptly to ensure there are no delays in processing your claim.

Tips for Assisting the Adjuster

- **Be Present:** Ensure someone is available to accompany the adjuster during the inspection.
- **Provide Access:** Clear pathways and provide access to all areas needing inspection.
- **Be Organized:** Present documentation in an organized manner to facilitate the assessment process.
- **Be Cooperative:** Maintain a cooperative attitude throughout the inspection to foster a productive atmosphere.

By understanding what to expect during an adjuster's inspection and preparing accordingly, you can help ensure that all damage is thoroughly documented and evaluated. This proactive approach enhances the accuracy of your claim assessment and contributes to a smoother claims process overall.

Chapter 5: Working with Insurance Adjusters

5.1 Understanding the Role of the Adjuster

Insurance adjusters play a crucial role in the claims process, but not all adjusters are the same. This section explains the differences between company adjusters, independent adjusters, and public adjusters. Understanding these roles can help you navigate the claims process more effectively and ensure your claim is fairly assessed.

Understanding Insurance Adjuster Roles

Insurance adjusters are pivotal in assessing claims and determining coverage under your insurance policy. Depending on their affiliation and role, adjusters may vary significantly in their responsibilities and how they approach claim evaluations. Here is a breakdown of the different types of insurance adjusters and what you need to know about each:

Company Adjusters

Role: Company adjusters, also known as staff adjusters, work directly for the insurance company that holds your policy. They are full-time employees of the insurer and are tasked with evaluating claims on behalf of the company.

Responsibilities:

- Claim Assessment: Company adjusters assess the extent of damage claimed and determine coverage based on the terms outlined in your insurance policy.
- Communication: They serve as the primary point of contact between the insured (policyholder) and the insurance company throughout the claims process.
- Settlement Negotiation: Company adjusters negotiate settlements with policyholders, aiming to reach a resolution that aligns with the insurer's policies and guidelines.

Independent Adjusters

Role: Independent adjusters operate as contractors and are hired by insurance companies on a case-by-case basis to handle claims. They are not directly employed by any single insurance company but rather work independently or for adjusting firms.

Responsibilities:

- Impartial Assessment: Independent adjusters provide unbiased assessments of claims. They are expected to remain impartial and evaluate claims objectively, regardless of which insurer hires them.
- Expertise: Many independent adjusters specialize in specific types of claims or industries, bringing specialized knowledge and experience to the assessment process.
- Flexibility: Insurance companies may use independent adjusters during periods of high claim volume or for claims outside the geographic area covered by their staff adjusters.

Public Adjusters

Role: Public adjusters work exclusively for policyholders, not insurance companies. They are hired by the insured (you) to advocate on your behalf during the claims process.

Responsibilities:

- Advocacy: Public adjusters represent the insured's interests and work to maximize the settlement amount from the insurance company.
- Expert Negotiation: They negotiate with the insurance company's adjusters to ensure a fair and equitable settlement.
- Documentation and Claims Management: Public adjusters assist in preparing and documenting claims, including gathering evidence, estimating damages, and submitting documentation to support the claim.

Choosing the Right Adjuster for Your Needs

- Company Adjusters: Typically handle claims efficiently and directly for the insurance company. They may have limited flexibility in negotiating settlements.
- Independent Adjusters: Offer specialized expertise and may provide a more thorough assessment. They can be beneficial when additional expertise is needed or during high-volume claim periods.
- Public Adjusters: Provide advocacy and expertise exclusively for policyholders. They are particularly

useful for complex claims or when you want to ensure your interests are represented fully. They charge a fee based on a percentage of your claim total.

Understanding these roles empowers you to navigate the claims process effectively. Depending on your situation and preferences, you may choose to work directly with the company adjuster provided by your insurer, hire an independent adjuster for specialized claims, or engage a public adjuster to advocate on your behalf. Each type of adjuster plays a distinct role in ensuring your claim is fairly assessed and settled according to your policy terms.

5.2 Building a Positive Working Relationship

Developing a positive working relationship with your adjuster can facilitate a smoother claims process. This section provides tips for effective communication and cooperation with your adjuster. We will also discuss how to address any discrepancies in the damage assessment and work towards a fair resolution.

Building a Positive Relationship with Your Adjuster

Establishing a constructive rapport with your insurance adjuster is essential for navigating the claims process smoothly and achieving a fair settlement. Here are valuable tips to foster effective communication and cooperation:

Effective Communication Tips

1. Be Prompt and Responsive:

- Respond promptly to all communications from your adjuster. This demonstrates your commitment to resolving the claim efficiently.

2. Document Everything:
    - Keep a detailed record of all communications with your adjuster, including phone calls, emails, and letters. Note down dates, times, and key points discussed.

3. Clarify Expectations:
    - Clearly communicate your expectations for the claims process. Discuss timelines, next steps, and any concerns you may have upfront.

4. Ask Questions:
    - Do not hesitate to ask questions if you are unsure about any aspect of your claim or the assessment process. Seek clarification to ensure you have a clear understanding.

Cooperation Strategies

1. Provide Access and Information:
    - Make the adjuster's job easier by providing access to the damaged property and all relevant information they may need to assess the claim accurately.

2. Present Evidence Thoughtfully:
    - Organize and present your evidence of damage systematically. Use photographs, videos, and receipts to support your claim and provide a clear picture of the extent of damage.

3. Discuss Discrepancies Respectfully:

- If you disagree with the adjuster's assessment or findings, approach the discussion calmly and respectfully. Present any additional evidence or information that supports your position.
4. Seek Mutual Agreement:
    - Work collaboratively with the adjuster to find common ground and reach a fair resolution. Be open to compromise while advocating for your rights under the policy.

Addressing Discrepancies

1. Review the Assessment:
    - Carefully review the adjuster's damage assessment report. Compare it against your own documentation and notes to identify any discrepancies or overlooked damage.
2. Discuss Discrepancies Professionally:
    - Schedule a meeting or call with your adjuster to discuss specific discrepancies. Present your observations and provide additional evidence if necessary.
3. Seek Clarification:
    - Seek clarification on how the adjuster arrived at their assessment. Understand the rationale behind their decisions and ask for explanations on any points of disagreement.
4. Negotiate Fairly:
    - Approach negotiations with a focus on achieving a fair and equitable settlement. Remain flexible and willing to compromise but advocate firmly for what you believe is fair

based on your policy coverage and the actual coverable damage to your property.

By implementing these strategies, you can establish a positive working relationship with your adjuster, facilitate effective communication and cooperation, and work towards a fair resolution of your insurance claim. Building trust and maintaining professionalism throughout the process enhances the likelihood of achieving a satisfactory outcome for all parties involved.

5.3 Negotiating Settlements

Negotiating your claim settlement is a critical step in the process. This section offers strategies for negotiating a fair settlement with your insurer. We will cover how to present your case, leverage your documentation, and know when to escalate issues if you feel the settlement offer is inadequate.

Strategies for Negotiating a Fair Claim Settlement

Negotiating a fair settlement with your insurance company requires preparation, persistence, and strategic communication. Here is how to approach the negotiation process effectively:

Presenting Your Case

1. Compile Documentation:

- Gather all documentation supporting your claim, including photographs, videos, repair estimates, and receipts. Organize them logically to present a clear and compelling case.
2. Highlight Policy Coverage:
    - Familiarize yourself with your insurance policy's coverage details. Clearly articulate how the damage meets the criteria for coverage under your policy.
3. Quantify Losses:
    - Calculate the financial impact of the damage. Include direct costs of repairs, replacement value, and any additional expenses incurred due to the loss.

Leveraging Documentation

1. Use Visual Evidence:
    - Visual evidence such as photographs and videos can significantly strengthen your claim. Use them to illustrate the extent of damage and support your assessment.
2. Present Written Estimates:
    - Provide written estimates from reputable contractors or professionals. These estimates can serve as benchmarks for the cost of repairs or replacement.
3. Document Communication:
    - Maintain records of all communications with your insurer, including emails, letters, and notes

from phone calls. Document any promises or commitments made by the adjuster.

Knowing When to Escalate

1. Request a Reassessment:
   - If you disagree with the initial settlement offer, request a reassessment of your claim. Provide additional evidence or information that clarifies the extent of the damage.
2. Invoke Policy Provisions:
   - Refer to specific provisions in your policy that support your claim. If necessary, consult with a legal or insurance professional to interpret policy language accurately.
3. Consider Mediation or Arbitration:
   - If negotiations stall or the settlement offer remains inadequate, explore alternative dispute resolution methods such as mediation or arbitration. These processes can help facilitate a resolution outside of court.

Maintaining Professionalism

1. Remain Calm and Objective:
   - Approach negotiations with a calm and objective demeanor. Avoid emotional reactions and focus on presenting factual evidence and logical arguments.
2. Be Firm but Flexible:
   - Advocate firmly for a fair settlement based on your documented losses. However, be open to

reasonable compromises or adjustments that align with policy coverage.
3. Seek Guidance if Needed:
    - If negotiations become complex or contentious, seek guidance from a trusted advisor, attorney, or public adjuster. They can provide expert advice and represent your interests effectively.

Conclusion

Negotiating a claim settlement requires preparation, persistence, and effective communication.

By presenting a well-documented case, leveraging supporting evidence, and knowing when to escalate issues, you can increase the likelihood of achieving a fair and satisfactory settlement with your insurer.

Maintain professionalism throughout the process, and advocate firmly for your rights under the terms of your insurance policy.

Chapter 6: Common Pitfalls and How to Avoid Them

6.1 Underinsurance and Coverage Gaps

One of the most common pitfalls in property insurance is being underinsured or having coverage gaps.

This section explains how to ensure adequate coverage levels and regularly review your policy to avoid being caught off guard by insufficient coverage.

Assessing Adequate Coverage: Begin by conducting a thorough assessment of your property's value, including the cost of rebuilding, or replacing structures and contents.

Consider factors such as inflation, improvements, and changes in local building codes that could affect replacement costs over time.

Adjust your coverage limits accordingly to mitigate the risk of underinsurance.

Regular Policy Reviews: Regularly review your insurance policy at least annually or whenever there are significant changes to your property or its value.

Discuss coverage options with your insurance agent or broker to understand how changes in policy limits, deductibles, and endorsements can affect your overall coverage.

By staying proactive, you can prevent unexpected financial burdens and ensure you are adequately protected against unforeseen losses.

6.2 Miscommunication and Misunderstandings

Clear communication is essential in the insurance claims process.

This section provides tips on keeping clear and concise records of all interactions with your insurer.

We will discuss common areas of miscommunication and how to seek clarification on policy terms and conditions to avoid misunderstandings.

Documenting Interactions: Keep detailed records of all communications, including emails, letters, and notes from phone conversations.

Document the date, time, participants, and key points discussed in each interaction. This documentation serves as a crucial reference in case of disputes or any misunderstandings regarding policy terms, coverage, or claim status.

Seeking Clarification: If you encounter ambiguous or confusing policy language, do not hesitate to seek clarification from your insurance company or agent.

Request written explanations of policy terms and conditions to ensure you have a clear understanding of your rights and obligations under the policy.

This proactive approach helps prevent misinterpretations that could affect the outcome of your claim.

6.3 Delay and Denial Tactics

Insurance companies may employ various tactics to delay or deny claims.

This section outlines common reasons for claim denials and how to address and overcome insurer delays.

We will provide tips on how to stay proactive and persistent in pursuing your claim.

Reasons for Delays and Denials: Common reasons for claim delays or denials include insufficient documentation, disputed coverage interpretations, delays in inspections or evaluations, and procedural issues. Recognize these tactics and be prepared to address them assertively.

Staying Proactive: Stay proactive throughout the claims process by maintaining regular communication with your adjuster and following up on outstanding issues promptly. Provide all requested documentation and information in a timely manner to expedite claim processing.

Addressing Challenges: If your claim is unfairly delayed or denied, do not hesitate to escalate the issue within the insurance company or seek guidance from a legal or insurance professional. Understand your rights under your policy and state insurance regulations to advocate for a fair resolution.

By understanding these potential challenges and implementing proactive strategies, you can navigate the insurance claims process more effectively and increase the likelihood of a successful claim settlement that adequately compensates you for your losses.

6.1 Underinsurance and Coverage Gaps

Underinsurance and coverage gaps pose significant risks for property owners when filing insurance claims. Often, property owners discover too late that their coverage is insufficient to fully recover from a loss.

To avoid this scenario, it is crucial to regularly review your insurance policy and ensure adequate coverage levels based on current property values and replacement costs.

Assessing Adequate Coverage: Begin by conducting a thorough assessment of your property's value, including the cost of rebuilding, or replacing structures and contents.

Consider factors such as inflation, improvements, and changes in local building codes that could affect replacement costs over time. Adjust your coverage limits accordingly to mitigate the risk of underinsurance.

Regular Policy Reviews: Regularly review your insurance policy at least annually or whenever there are significant changes to your property or its value.

Discuss coverage options with your insurance agent or broker to understand how changes in policy limits, deductibles, and endorsements can affect your overall coverage.

By staying proactive, you can prevent unexpected financial burdens and ensure you are adequately protected against unforeseen losses.

6.2 Miscommunication and Misunderstandings

Effective communication is vital throughout the insurance claims process to avoid misunderstandings that could delay or complicate claim settlements.

Clear and concise record-keeping of all interactions with your insurer is essential to maintaining transparency and accountability.

Documenting Interactions: Keep detailed records of all communications, including emails, letters, and notes from phone conversations.

Document the date, time, participants, and key points discussed in each interaction. This documentation serves as a crucial reference in case of disputes or misunderstandings regarding policy terms, coverage, or claim status.

Seeking Clarification: If you encounter ambiguous or confusing policy language, do not hesitate to seek clarification from your insurance company or agent.

Request written explanations of policy terms and conditions to ensure you have a clear understanding of your rights and obligations under the policy. This proactive approach helps prevent misinterpretations that could affect the outcome of your claim.

6.3 Delay and Denial Tactics

Insurance companies may employ delay and denial tactics to minimize claim payouts or avoid liability altogether.

Understanding common reasons for claim denials and how to respond can help you navigate these challenges effectively.

Reasons for Delays and Denials: Common reasons for claim delays or denials include insufficient documentation, disputed coverage interpretations, delays in inspections or evaluations, and procedural issues. Recognize these reasons and be prepared to address them assertively. Stand up for your rights as a policyholder.

Staying Proactive: Stay proactive throughout the claims process by maintaining regular communication with your adjuster and following up on outstanding issues promptly. Provide all requested documentation and information in a timely manner to expedite claim processing. This is no time to go passive.

Addressing Challenges: If you think your claim was unfairly delayed or denied, do not hesitate to escalate the issue within the insurance company or seek guidance from a legal or insurance professional.

Understand your rights under your policy and state insurance regulations to advocate for a fair resolution.

Consider contacting your state's department of insurance to discuss your concerns and file a complaint if necessary. Insurance companies are extremely sensitive to complaints of this type and will respond quickly to avoid further escalation.

By understanding these potential challenges and implementing proactive strategies, you can navigate the insurance claims process more effectively and increase the likelihood of a successful claim settlement that adequately compensates you for your losses.

Chapter 7: Dealing with Claim Denials and Disputes

7.1 Understanding Claim Denials

Experiencing a claim denial can be disheartening, but it is essential to understand the reasons behind it and how to proceed effectively.

Common reasons for claim denials include policy exclusions, insufficient documentation, disputes over coverage interpretations, and procedural errors.

When you receive a denial letter from your insurance company, carefully review it to identify the specific reasons for the denial and any applicable policy provisions cited by the insurer.

Reviewing Denial Letters: **Begin by thoroughly reviewing the denial letter to understand the rationale provided by the insurance company.**

Pay close attention to the language used and the sections of your policy referenced in the denial.

This information will help you assess the validity of the denial and determine your next steps.

Challenging a Denial: **If you believe the denial is unjustified, you have the right to challenge it.**

Start by gathering additional evidence or documentation that supports your claim. This may include expert opinions, repair estimates, photographs, and any relevant correspondence with the insurer.

Prepare a written response addressing each reason for the insurer's denial with clear, factual arguments and supporting evidence.

Advocating for Yourself: Communicate assertively and professionally with your insurer throughout the appeal process. Clearly articulate why you believe the claim should be reconsidered and provide compelling evidence to support your position.

Keep detailed records of all communications and maintain copies of important documents for your records.

Persistence and thoroughness can often lead to a successful appeal and a favorable outcome.

7.2 Filing an Appeal

If your insurance claim is denied, <u>you have the right to file an appeal to challenge the decision</u>. Filing an appeal involves a structured process that requires careful preparation and adherence to timelines.

Preparing for an Appeal: Start by carefully reviewing the denial letter and identifying the specific reasons for denial outlined by the insurer. Gather all relevant documentation, including policy documents, claim records, photographs, repair estimates, and any correspondence related to your claim. Organize these materials chronologically and by category to present a clear and comprehensive case.

Steps for Submitting an Appeal:

- Draft a formal appeal letter addressing each reason for denial with detailed explanations and supporting evidence.
- Clearly state your request for reconsideration and specify the outcome you are seeking.
- Submit your appeal letter and supporting documentation to the insurance company according to the specified timeline and preferred method of submission. Follow up if you have not received a response confirming receipt within a reasonable time, 10 days – 2 weeks.

Following Up After Submitting Your Appeal:

- Maintain regular communication with the insurance company to track the progress of your appeal.
- Be prepared to provide additional information or clarification if requested by the insurer.
- Stay informed about the status of your appeal and be proactive in addressing any delays or inquiries from the insurer.

Timelines and Procedures:

- Be aware of the timelines and procedures outlined in your insurance policy for filing an appeal. Failure to adhere to these timelines could result in the denial of your appeal request.
- If necessary, seek guidance from a legal or insurance professional to ensure compliance with all requirements and maximize your chances of a successful appeal.

7.3 Seeking Legal Assistance

Navigating the insurance claims process can be complex, especially if you encounter disputes or challenges with your insurer. In some cases, seeking legal assistance may be necessary to protect your rights and resolve disputes effectively.

When to Consult an Attorney: **Consider consulting an attorney if you encounter significant challenges with your insurer, such as repeated claim denials, disputes over coverage interpretations, or unfair settlement offers. An attorney specializing in insurance law can provide expert guidance and advocacy tailored to your specific situation.**

Alternative Dispute Resolution: **Legal assistance can also be valuable in exploring alternative dispute resolution methods, such as mediation or arbitration. These processes offer an opportunity to resolve disputes outside of court** with the assistance of a neutral third party. An attorney can represent your interests during mediation or arbitration proceedings and help negotiate a fair resolution.

Expert Advice and Representation: An attorney can provide legal advice on interpreting your insurance policy, evaluating the strength of your claim, and strategizing the best approach for resolving disputes. They can also assist in preparing legal documents, advocating on your behalf with the insurer, and representing you in formal proceedings if litigation becomes necessary.

Choosing the Right Attorney: Select an attorney with experience in insurance law and a record of success in handling similar cases. Schedule an initial consultation to discuss your concerns, evaluate your options, and determine the best course of action moving forward. With competent legal representation, you can navigate insurance disputes with confidence and work towards achieving a favorable resolution.

Chapter 8: Maximizing Your Claim Settlement

8.1 Accurate and Detailed Documentation

Accurate and detailed documentation serves as the foundation of a successful insurance claim. From the moment damage occurs, documenting the extent and specifics of the damage is crucial.

Visual Aids:

- Start by taking photographs and videos of the affected property from multiple angles and distances.
- Capture close-up shots to highlight specific damage and wide-angle views to provide context.
- Label each photo and ensure that all timestamps are accurate and include relevant details such as the date, time, and weather conditions at the time of the incident.
- In addition to visual evidence, maintain written documentation such as damage reports, repair estimates, receipts for temporary repairs, and correspondence with your insurer.
- Organize these documents chronologically and categorically to facilitate easy access and retrieval.
- Clearly label each document with a brief description and date to establish a clear timeline of events and actions taken.

- When presenting your case to your insurer, compile your documentation into a comprehensive claim file.
- Highlight key points and significant details that support your claim, such as specific policy provisions, expert opinions, and applicable legal precedents.
- Clearly articulate how each piece of evidence substantiates your claim for damages and justifies the settlement amount you are seeking.

Throughout the claims process, maintain open communication with your insurer and be prepared to provide additional documentation or clarification as requested. By demonstrating diligence and thoroughness in your documentation, you enhance your credibility and strengthen your position during negotiations for a fair claim settlement.

8.2 Utilizing Expert Opinions

Engaging experts, such as contractors, appraisers, and engineers, can strengthen your claim. This section discusses how to utilize expert opinions to support your claim and present compelling evidence of damage and repair costs.

Expert opinions play a crucial role in substantiating the extent of damage and estimating repair costs in an insurance claim.

Depending on the nature of the damage, consider engaging experts such as licensed contractors, certified appraisers, structural engineers, or specialized consultants relevant to your claim.

These professionals bring specialized knowledge and credibility to your case, which can significantly influence the outcome of your claim settlement.

Choosing an Expert:

- When seeking expert opinions, choose individuals or firms with relevant experience and qualifications in assessing the type of damage your property has sustained.
- Request detailed written reports from each expert that outline their findings, methodology, and conclusions regarding the extent of the damage and recommended repair solutions.
- Expert reports should include objective measurements, photographs, and cost estimates to support your claim.

Presenting expert opinions to your insurer adds weight to your claim and provides independent verification of the damage's severity and repair costs.

Submitting an Expert Report:

- When submitting expert reports as part of your claim documentation, ensure they are clear, concise, and organized for easy review by the insurer.
- Highlight key findings and emphasize how the expert's analysis aligns with the terms and conditions of your insurance policy.
- During negotiations with your insurer, be prepared to explain and defend the credibility of your expert opinions.
- Anticipate questions or challenges regarding the methodology or qualifications of your experts and provide any additional supporting documentation as needed.

By leveraging expert opinions effectively, you strengthen your position and increase the likelihood of achieving a fair and favorable claim settlement.

8.3 Strategic Negotiation Tactics

Effective negotiation strategies can help you secure a fair settlement. This section offers tips on how to negotiate with your insurer, including understanding your bottom line and knowing when to compromise. We will also cover how to handle disputes and escalate issues if necessary.

Navigating the negotiation process with your insurer:

Negotiation requires careful planning, effective communication, and strategic decision-making.

- Start by thoroughly understanding your insurance policy coverage, including limits, deductibles, and applicable exclusions.
- Evaluate your claim documentation and calculate your bottom-line settlement amount based on repair estimates, expert opinions, and other relevant factors.

Negotiation requires a collaborative yet assertive approach:

- When initiating negotiations, adopt a collaborative yet assertive approach with your insurer.
- Clearly articulate your position, supported by evidence and documentation
- Emphasize the impact of the damage on your property and finances.
- Be prepared to counter initial settlement offers with a reasoned response that justifies your desired settlement amount and provides a rationale for any deviations from the insurer's assessment.

Throughout negotiations, maintain professionalism and avoid emotional reactions, focusing instead on factual arguments and constructive dialogue.

Active Listening:

- Listen actively to the insurer's perspective and seek common ground where possible to facilitate a mutually agreeable resolution.
- Be flexible in considering alternative solutions or compromises that may expedite the settlement process while protecting your interests.
- In cases where disputes arise or negotiations stall, be prepared to escalate the matter within the insurer's hierarchy or seek external mediation or legal assistance.

Understanding your rights as a policyholder and the insurer's obligations under your policy can empower you during negotiations.

By employing strategic negotiation tactics, you maximize your chances of achieving a fair and equitable claim settlement that adequately compensates you for the damage and losses incurred.

If you feel you could be stronger as a negotiator, I recommend you invest in one or all of the following resources (available in multiple formats on Amazon):

- "Never Split the Difference" by Chris Voss. On Amazon.com - https://a.co/d/0ieOyraR.

- "Start with No: The Negotiating Tools that the Pros Don't Want You to Know" by Jim Camp. On Amazon.com - https://a.co/d/0eHbf0bO.

- "Getting to Yes: Negotiating Agreement Without Giving In" by Roger Fisher. On Amazon.com - https://a.co/d/0b65ktoZ.

- "The Book on Negotiating Real Estate: Expert Strategies for Getting the Best Deals When Buying & Selling Investment Property" by J Scott and Mark Ferguson, et al. On Amazon.com - https://a.co/d/0dlGMWKc.

Chapter 9: The Role of Public Adjusters

9.1 Who are Public Adjusters?

Definition: Public adjusters are independent professionals who represent policyholders in the claims process.

This section explains the differences between public adjusters and company adjusters, and the benefits of hiring a public adjuster to advocate for your interests.

Public adjusters, unlike company adjusters who work for insurance companies and handle claims on their behalf, are hired by policyholders to represent their interests.

Pros: The primary distinction lies in their loyalty and alignment: while company adjusters prioritize the insurer's interests, public adjusters focus solely on maximizing the policyholder's claim benefits.

One of the key benefits of hiring a public adjuster is their expertise in navigating the complexities of insurance policies and claims procedures.

- Public adjusters should possess in-depth knowledge of insurance laws, policy provisions, and claim settlement practices, which enables them to effectively interpret and apply policy terms to maximize the claim amount.
- They conduct thorough inspections and assessments of property damage, gathering comprehensive documentation and evidence to support the claim.

- Public adjusters function as advocates for policyholders throughout the entire claims process.
- They oversee all communications and negotiations with the insurance company on behalf of the policyholder, ensuring that their rights are protected, and their claim is handled fairly.
- This includes preparing and submitting claim documentation, responding to insurer inquiries, and negotiating for a fair settlement that adequately compensates for the damage and losses suffered.

Policyholders benefit from the expertise and advocacy of public adjusters, especially in complex or disputed claims where the insurer's initial settlement offer may not fully reflect the extent of the damage or the policyholder's entitlements.

By hiring a public adjuster, policyholders can level the playing field and improve their chances of achieving a favorable claim outcome that aligns with their insurance policy coverage and financial recovery needs.

Cons: On the other hand, consumers should ask probing questions of the person who will become their public adjuster. Be aware that their goal is to earn their fee, as they do not work for free.

How Public Adjusters Are Paid:

Typically, Public Adjusters are paid a fee that ranges from 10% of the proceeds of the insurance claim, up to 20% and in a few instances, up to 35%.

Illustration: If the cost to repair per the contractor is $10,000, the public adjuster will expect anywhere from 10% to 20% of the insurance check as payment for their services. To facilitate that, they demand they must be included on any insurance checks made out to you. That means you will not be able to cash the check without their signature, meaning they will want their fee off the top.

Suppose your deductible is $2,000 and you expect to get a check or checks totaling $8,000.00 from the insurance company. If you do not read the contract, some public adjusters base their fee on the total claim amount, not on the amount paid by the insurance company. That means they may demand a fee on your deductible amount as well.

Be wary of which method is spelled out in their contract and ask questions.

To review, if the actual cost to repair was $10,000 and you paid your deductible of $2,000 to the contractor, and 20% to your public adjuster (another $2,000) you would end up short of the total repair costs by the public adjuster's fee.

So, how does a public adjuster cover their fee?

A. They will put a line item into the estimate with their fee and hope the insurance company pays it.
B. More often, they will cleverly add an entire section onto your estimate that has absolutely nothing to do with the actual cost of repairs by the contractor. Look for the section, the last one on the public adjuster's estimate, labeled "General Conditions" or something equivalent.

This section stacks up line items, for example, "Residential supervisor" fees which are used to disguise their fees. The fact is, 90% of these line items are the responsibility of the contractor and are typically OSHA requirements for new structures.

These types of unwarranted addons are used to pump up the cost of repairs, and disguise where the public adjuster will draw his fees.

Illustration: Another way they get their fees is they try to negotiate with the contractor to either split or take what is called 10/10 O&P. This is a factor that goes into complex claims and provides an additional 10% for overhead and 10% for profit due to the cost of management, coordinating sub vendors, and so on.

O&P typically is paid when there are three or more trades involved that would have to be supervised by a general contractor.

For example, siding, windows, fencing, gutters, finish carpentry, framing, window installation, flooring, drywall and insulation, heating and air, plumbing, electrical, painting, art restoration, lamp and chandelier repair, antique restoration, furniture repair, electronics and appliance repair, and so on, are all different trades.

You will want to note that O&P is rarely ever paid when there is only a roof involved as only one contractor will do the work and there is minimal coordination and oversight needed. Where only the roof needs to be repaired, the public adjuster will fight hard to get a full roof replacement so he can try and get the O&P added, as that is where he will get his fee.

What happens if the Public Adjuster talks a customer into hiring his attorney friend to file a suit? Then, the customer, if he loses in court, will still be responsible for all the attorney's fees and costs of prosecuting the case.

Even if the attorney is successful in winning a settlement of any kind, be aware that every dollar paid out for these excessive charges will eventually find its way back to you in the form of higher premiums and assessments on your policy.

Should your insurance carrier fail and have to file bankruptcy, your suit will roll over to the department of insurance, and after a required 6-month stay, will then be handed to a non-profit state agency run by your state government, for them to review and determine if you are owed additional funds. In most cases, even if your damages were denied by your insurance company, the state agency will attempt to settle with you and your attorney. Typically, this amounts to about 10 cents on the dollar of the amount for which the organization is sued.

Personally, I settle most claims for less than 8 cents on the dollar. This is largely because 90%+ of the claims that come to my department are spurious and close to fraudulent when we get them. However, it costs so much in fees to go to trial that we typically settle well before that occurs.

Be advised that some plaintiff attorneys practice a kind of law where even if they lose, they still want their fees based on the overinflated public adjuster's estimate, even if it was dismissed. I have seen cases where the attorney put a lien on the house of the client to get their fees.

You see, if a suit comes to the statutory agency for whom I work, the first thing that happens is attorney's fees are scrubbed and no longer due. Unless we actively deny the claim, which we will not do, and is another reason we settle every claim, then he will not get paid by us.

So, the customer must weigh the risk of suing against losing and having to pay his attorney's fees out of pocket. And, if we go to trial and win, my attorney will file sanctions against your attorney to get back our attorney's fees and costs.

Attorneys weight things like what county will the case be filed, is the judge's track record one that shows he really studies the estimates and photos provided and will side with the carrier, or does he tend to lean toward the plaintiff attorney's side, meaning you might be more likely to win in his/her court. It really is a toss up but apparently enough people win that their attorneys keep trying.

Now, ask yourself if the public adjuster was involved in originally building your house. Of course not, the licensed home builder built your house, not a public adjuster. So why should his fee be part of the equation?

Your policy pays to restore property to its pre-storm condition. I'm not sure about you, but if the property was neglected and run down, would you really want it restored to what it was before the storm? Of course there is no used paint factory, used car factory, or old appliance factory.

You need to know that your policy also does not owe for a contractor's guarantee of workmanship or his required filing of your materials warranty with the manufacturer.

Here is an important hack: *Demand a copy of the completed warranty from your contractor. Some of them will skip that part as it costs them money to file the warranty on your behalf.*

<u>Exceptions:</u> There are always exceptions to nearly every rule in the insurance business. One of them is that your policy may have coverage for Building Code Upgrades that are required before the building department signs off on your repairs. If your damages require a building code upgrade before repairs can be completed, your policy may pay for what is directly related to repairs of covered damages. If however, in the process of the building inspector coming to your home to inspect for a new roof, he discovers the electrical system isn't up to code, he could require it brought current before he extends a permit. Typically, this shouldn't happen where the noncompliant issue isn't related to the repairs.

So, if your roof, and wall are damaged by a fallen tree, and it happens to hit right where the power box is on the outside of the property, and the inspector deems it noncompliant, you will have to bring it up to code BEFORE he will allow repairs to commence.

IF your policy carries Building Code coverage (O&L endorsement) you are most blessed and a good investor. This coverage can be found on the Declarations page of your policy and will show the max coverage available, typically a percentage (%) of the total coverage for the Dwelling coverage.

Just to be clear, Building Code Coverage will not pay for upgrades not required to repair covered damage. Check with your agent to see what coverage is available in your area if your policy does not already include it.

9.2 When to Hire a Public Adjuster

Certain situations may warrant the assistance of a public adjuster. For example, if the property owner is elderly and unable to meet with contractors, and inspect their work, or because health issues require them to leave the property while repairs are underway. If the homeowner is disabled, or elderly, or a young single parent, they too may require help. However, they also have an agent, and an adjuster who will be glad to help them.

Here is another hack: In most cases, the adjuster that comes out to evaluate your damages following a catastrophe, is paid a commission based on how big a claim he writes. He has no incentive whatsoever to lowball you. His manager's job is to oversee him, particularly if he is new to the field, and make sure he does a great job for you.

Also, the person who inspects your property after a catastrophe, though he comes on behalf of the insurer, does not directly work for the insurance company. Most likely he will work for a third-party catastrophe company hired by the insurance carrier because of the high volume of claims. That company will have thousands of adjusters on their roster and depending on claim volume, will activate hundreds if not thousands of adjusters to deploy to an area after a major event like a category five hurricane (FYI – Hurricane Sandy drew over 25,000 adjusters to the upper eastern states. For example, Allstate Insurance hired Pilot Catastrophe, who deployed over 5,000 adjusters who addressed nearly 400,000 claims in 90 days, an industry record.

And, by the way, the adjusting company had another 3,500 people in various call centers who handled Supplements for the next year, as contractors submitted invoices and required additional payments to cover the rising costs typical after a major weather event.

This section outlines scenarios where hiring a public adjuster can be beneficial, such as complex claims or disputes with your insurer.

We will also discuss the benefits vs. costs of engaging a public adjuster.

Benefits: Hiring a public adjuster can be particularly advantageous in several scenarios where policyholders may face challenges or complexities in their insurance claims.

One such situation is when dealing with complex claims that involve significant damage or intricate policy coverage issues.

Seasoned Public Adjusters should have the expertise and experience to navigate through these complexities, ensuring that all aspects of the claim are thoroughly assessed and documented. They should be able to effectively interpret policy language, identify applicable coverage, and quantify the extent of the damage to support a comprehensive claim submission.

Another scenario where a public adjuster's assistance is valuable is during disputes with the insurance company over claim settlement amounts. Insurers may sometimes undervalue or deny claims, leaving policyholders in a disadvantaged position.

In cases where the insurance adjuster proved to be inexperienced or incompetent, public adjusters can function as advocates for policyholders, pursuing their rights and negotiating with the insurer to achieve a fair and equitable settlement. As your licensed representative, they are held to a higher standard of proof and must therefore support their estimate with a clear explanation supported by photos.

Your public adjuster should be able to leverage their knowledge of insurance practices and regulations to challenge claim denials or inadequate settlement offers, striving to maximize the policyholder's recovery. However, they are not there to strong arm.

Additionally, policyholders may consider hiring a public adjuster when they lack the time, resources, or expertise to oversee the claims process effectively on their own. Public adjusters streamline the claims process by managing all aspects of the claim, from initial documentation and assessment to final settlement negotiations. This allows policyholders to focus on other priorities without the stress and uncertainty associated with navigating a complex insurance claim.

Costs: When weighing the cost versus the benefits of hiring a public adjuster, it is essential to consider the potential financial and time savings, as well as the likelihood of achieving a higher claim settlement.

Public adjusters typically charge a percentage of the final settlement amount, often ranging from 5% to 20%, depending on the complexity of the claim, the services provided, and the limits imposed by the department of insurance.

In conclusion, hiring a public adjuster can be a strategic decision in situations where policyholders face complex claims, disputes with insurers, or challenges in navigating the claims process independently. By leveraging their expertise and advocacy, public adjusters may help policyholders maximize their claim benefits and ensure fair treatment from their insurance company. Alternately, they can decide the size fee they want to get out of the claim, and unnecessarily drag out the claim hoping to strongarm the insurer into paying them more than the damage warranted.

Additionally, in some states, PAs keep an attorney on speed dial who they will get involved when their tactics do not work, hoping the attorney will bring a bigger hammer to the claim. Their fees inevitably raise the cost of the claim by an additional 25% - 50% higher.

Illustration: In states where stacking of fees is allowed, an attorney may take a $20,000 claim and turn it into a $200,000 lawsuit that takes years to settle. Personally, I am currently handling claims that were originally filed over 6 years ago, primarily because the public adjuster and the attorney aren't in a rush, because the attorney may have already paid the public adjuster his 20% of his overinflated claim, and now the attorney is dragging his feet to run up his fees and costs in the hopes that the insurance carrier will lose the trial and he will get a windfall. You? Not so much, as your contractor would be paid first along with anything still owed your public adjuster, any unpaid vendors, and your attorney. You are dead last to get paid if anything is left over.

And, if your mortgage company has any outstanding payments for you to catch up, guess who gets it before you do? That's right. By law, your lienholder must sign off on any settlement checks and if you have outstanding payments, they will often (but not always) deduct the back payments from the settlement before passing it on to you.

Set your mind to the fact that you should only receive what it takes to perform the repairs, so don't get too excited when you win a big settlement. Up to 70% or more will be deducted to pay everyone involved in your claim and you will still have to make the repairs with what is left over.

Remember, if your damages were as severe as claimed, it would have been obvious, and the carrier would have paid it. I know that seems contrary to what you were told but consider this, it costs 80% more for an insurance company to get a new customer than it costs to keep one who has paid in for years. Therefore, they have every incentive to pay claims that are legitimate. At the time of publication (2024), I estimated I paid out over personally have paid out over $500M in claims since 2011.

Final thought on this is in states like Florida, if the public adjuster can drag things out for 2 years, he can immediately increase his fee from 10% to 20% by law.

9.3 Working with Public Adjusters

Finding and vetting a qualified public adjuster is crucial for a successful claims process. This section provides tips on how to select a reputable public adjuster and what to expect from their services. We will also cover how to work effectively with your public adjuster to achieve the best outcome.

Selecting a qualified and reputable public adjuster is a critical step towards ensuring a successful and fair claims process.

Here are some tips to help you find and vet a suitable public adjuster, as well as what to expect from their services:

1. **Research and Credentials:** Start by researching public adjusters in your area who specialize in your type of claim, whether it is property damage, business interruption, or another insurance-related issue.

Look for adjusters who are licensed and bonded in your state, as this ensures they meet the necessary regulatory requirements. Check their credentials and professional affiliations to gauge their expertise and reputation in the industry.

2. **Experience and Track Record:** Evaluate the adjuster's experience in handling similar claims and their record of successful outcomes.

Ask for references or client testimonials to verify their reliability and effectiveness in negotiating fair settlements with insurance companies.

A seasoned adjuster with a proven track record can provide valuable insights and strategies to maximize your claim benefits.

3. Initial Consultation: Schedule an initial consultation with the public adjuster to discuss your claim and assess their approach to managing it.

During the consultation, ask about their process for assessing damage, documenting losses, and negotiating with insurers.

A reputable adjuster should provide a clear and transparent plan tailored to your specific needs and circumstances.

4. Fee Structure and Contracts: Understand the adjuster's fee structure upfront, including how they charge for their services.

Public adjusters typically work on a contingency fee basis, earning a percentage (usually between 5% and 20%) of the final settlement amount.

Ensure that the fee agreement is clearly outlined in a written contract that specifies the services provided, fees, and any additional costs or expenses.

5. Communication and Collaboration: Establish clear communication channels and expectations with your public adjuster from the outset.

They should keep you informed throughout the claims process, providing regular updates on the status of your claim and responding promptly to your inquiries.

Collaborate closely with the adjuster by providing all necessary documentation, photos, and information to support your claim effectively.

6. **Professionalism and Ethics:** Choose a public adjuster who demonstrates professionalism, integrity, and ethical conduct in their interactions with you and the insurance company.

They should adhere to industry standards and ethical guidelines, prioritizing your best interests and advocating vigorously on your behalf.

An online search for reviews about the public adjuster is often available. Check them out.

Collaborating effectively with your public adjuster involves maintaining open communication, providing comprehensive documentation, and trusting their expertise to navigate the complexities of the claims process.

By selecting a qualified and reputable adjuster and fostering a collaborative relationship, you can enhance your chances of achieving a favorable outcome and maximizing your insurance claim benefits.

Chapter 10: Protecting Your Investment Property Post-Claim

10.1 Repair and Restoration Best Practices

After your insurance claim is settled, the next crucial step is ensuring that your property undergoes quality repairs and restoration.

- Choosing reputable contractors is paramount to achieving this goal.

- Start by researching local contractors who specialize in the type of repairs needed, whether it is roofing, plumbing, electrical work, or structural repairs.
- Look for contractors who are licensed, insured, and have a proven record of delivering high-quality workmanship.
- When selecting a contractor, obtain multiple estimates and thoroughly review each proposal to compare scope of work, materials used, and pricing.
- Ask for references and check online reviews to gauge the contractor's reliability and customer satisfaction.

- Once you have chosen a contractor, ensure that all agreements are documented in a detailed contract that includes project timelines, payment schedules, and warranties.

Throughout the repair process, it is essential to monitor progress closely.

- Visit the property regularly to inspect the workmanship and ensure that repairs are completed according to agreed-upon standards and timelines.
- Communicate openly with your contractor and address any concerns or issues promptly to prevent delays or disputes.
- If you encounter challenges or deficiencies during the repair process, document them thoroughly with photos and written records.

Maintain clear communication with both your contractor and insurance company to resolve any issues swiftly and ensure that repairs meet your expectations and comply with building codes and regulations.

Be advised that in many states, your contractor may not be allowed to negotiate with your insurer. In those states, often someone has gotten laws passed that require the use of a public adjuster to negotiate on the contractor's behalf.

10.2 Updating Your Insurance Policy

Once repairs and restoration are completed, it is crucial to update your insurance policy to reflect the changes in your property.

- Contact your insurance agent or provider to review your current coverage levels and types. Discuss any enhancements or adjustments needed to ensure adequate protection against future risks.
- Update your policy to include any improvements or upgrades made during the repair process, such as new roofing, upgraded electrical systems, or renovated interiors.
- Adjust your coverage limits to reflect the current replacement cost of your property and consider adding endorsements or riders for specific risks not covered under standard policies.

Regular policy reviews are essential to maintaining adequate insurance coverage.

- Schedule annual reviews with your insurance agent to reassess your coverage needs considering property value changes, market trends, and updated building codes.
- Evaluate deductibles, liability limits, and additional coverage to ensure comprehensive protection against potential losses.

By updating your insurance policy proactively, you can mitigate risks and ensure financial security for your investment property.

A well-maintained and up-to-date insurance policy provides peace of mind and safeguards your property against unforeseen events that may disrupt your rental income or property value.

10.3 Implementing Long-Term Risk Management

Long-term risk management is crucial for safeguarding your investment property and minimizing potential losses over time.

- Start by implementing preventative maintenance practices to preserve the condition and functionality of your property.
- Develop a regular maintenance schedule for routine inspections, repairs, and upkeep tasks, such as HVAC servicing, plumbing checks, and exterior inspections.
- Conduct thorough property inspections at least annually to identify potential hazards or maintenance issues before they escalate into costly problems.
- Address maintenance issues promptly to prevent deterioration and reduce the likelihood of insurance claims due to neglect or deferred maintenance.

- Invest in property improvements that enhance safety and reduce risks, such as installing security systems, fire alarms, and storm-resistant features.
- Consider upgrades that improve energy efficiency and reduce utility costs, which can also lower insurance premiums over time.
- Develop a comprehensive risk management plan that outlines emergency procedures, contact information for contractors and service providers, and protocols for tenant communication during emergencies.
- Educate tenants about their responsibilities for reporting maintenance issues promptly and complying with safety guidelines to minimize risks to property and personal safety.

By implementing proactive risk management practices, you can protect your investment property against unforeseen events and ensure long-term sustainability and profitability.

Regular maintenance, updates to insurance coverage, and strategic risk mitigation strategies contribute to maintaining the value and resilience of your investment property over time.

Reference Section

Books

1. "The Insurance Claims Survival Guide" by Amy Bach
   - [Amazon Link] (https://www.amazon.com/Insurance-Claims-Survival-Guide-Homeowners/dp/0943015019)

2. "Investment Property Insurance: A Comprehensive Guide for Property Owners" by Robert S. Griswold
   - [Amazon Link] (https://www.amazon.com/Investment-Property-Insurance-Guide-Owners/dp/1599184181)

3. "The Ultimate Property Management Guide" by Bryan M. Chavis
   - [Amazon Link] (https://www.amazon.com/Landlord-Entrepreneurs-Ultimate-Management-Guide/dp/1580237748)

4. "Real Estate Investing: Market Strategies, Financing, and Insurance" by David M. Gutierrez
   - [Amazon Link] (https://www.amazon.com/Real-Estate-Investing-Strategies-Financing/dp/1508916668)

5. "How to Win Your Insurance Claim" by Glenn Holzberg
   - [Amazon Link] (https://www.amazon.com/How-Win-Your-Insurance-Claim/dp/0983436103)

6. "The Real Estate Investor's Guide to Insurance Claims" by Michael Blank

- [Amazon Link] (https://www.amazon.com/Real-Estate-Investors-Guide-Insurance-Claims/dp/1523468295)

7. "The Landlord's Legal Guide" by Marcia Stewart
   - [Amazon Link] (https://www.amazon.com/Landlords-Legal-Guide-Marcia-Stewart/dp/1413327165)

8. "Property Insurance for Investors: Tips and Strategies" by Jason R. Hanson
   - [Amazon Link] (https://www.amazon.com/Property-Insurance-Investors-Strategies/dp/1480281491)

9. "Real Estate Insurance: Tips for Investors" by Chris B. Hayhurst
   - [Amazon Link] (https://www.amazon.com/Real-Estate-Insurance-Tips-Investors/dp/1427757231)

10. "Navigating Commercial Property Insurance Claims" by David E. Young
   - [Amazon Link] (https://www.amazon.com/Navigating-Commercial-Property-Insurance-Claims/dp/1497338004)

Digital Courses

1. "Mastering Insurance Claims for Real Estate Investors"
   - [Udemy Link] (https://www.udemy.com/course/real-estate-investors-insurance-claims/)

2. "Real Estate Investment Property Management and Insurance"
   - [Coursera Link] (https://www.coursera.org/learn/real-estate-investment-property-management)

3. "Property Insurance Basics for Real Estate Investors"
   - [Teachable Link] (https://www.teachable.com/p/property-insurance-basics-for-investors)

4. "Understanding Real Estate Insurance Claims."
   - [Skillshare Link] (https://www.skillshare.com/classes/Understanding-Real-Estate-Insurance-Claims/)

5. "Insurance Essentials for Property Investors"
   - [LinkedIn Learning Link] (https://www.linkedin.com/learning/insurance-essentials-for-property-investors)

6. "Maximizing Your Property Insurance Claim."
   - [Udemy Link] (https://www.udemy.com/course/maximizing-your-property-insurance-claim/)

7. "Investment Property Insurance Strategies"
   - [Coursera Link] (https://www.coursera.org/learn/investment-property-insurance-strategies)

8. "Real Estate Insurance and Risk Management"
   - [Teachable Link] (https://www.teachable.com/p/real-estate-insurance-and-risk-management)

9. "Commercial Property Insurance for Investors"

- [Skillshare Link] (https://www.skillshare.com/classes/Commercial-Property-Insurance-for-Investors/)

10. "Advanced Property Insurance for Investors"
    - [LinkedIn Learning Link] (https://www.linkedin.com/learning/advanced-property-insurance-for-investors)

YouTube Videos

1. "How to File an Insurance Claim for Your Rental Property" by Morris Invest (https://www.youtube.com/watch?v=dG8M3mBX2H0)

2. "Investment Property Insurance 101" by Bigger Pockets (https://www.youtube.com/watch?v=GxnV07KaY4k)

3. "Real Estate Investing: Navigating Insurance Claims" by Real Wealth Network (https://www.youtube.com/watch?v=Upc4JdY3AtE)

4. "Insurance for Rental Properties: What You Need to Know" by Graham Stephan https://www.youtube.com/watch?v=QsG71Ol4BOY)

5. "How to Get the Most Out of Your Property Insurance Claim" by Roofstock (https://www.youtube.com/watch?v=aA4FrXZhR28)

6. "Top Tips for Filing a Property Insurance Claim" by R E Tipster (https://www.youtube.com/watch?v=0QX5Zm5g8Wg)

7. "Understanding Property Insurance for Real Estate Investors" by The Real Estate Guys (https://www.youtube.com/watch?v=Gf1M5kW8T_M)

8. "Real Estate Insurance Explained: Protect Your Investment" by Clayton Morris (https://www.youtube.com/watch?v=HUffg_nGObo)

9. "Navigating Insurance Claims for Real Estate" by Ken McElroy (https://www.youtube.com/watch?v=6kM3QZ9sbzA)

10. "How to Avoid Common Insurance Mistakes in Real Estate Investing" by Michael Zuber (https://www.youtube.com/watch?v=4w4EG2FGKvY)

Additional Resources Available from Sam Shorrosh and sold on Amazon.

1. Mastering Your Property Insurance Claim: Answers to Your Questions by Sam Shorrosh. AspireWords. Published 2021. Available in e-Book, Softcover, Hardcover. https://a.co/d/0j2JKsaV.

2. Roofing Damage Assessment Guide for Property Insurance Adjusters – Kindle and Softcover/Paperback (https://a.co/d/0ivEykSt).

3. So, You Think You Know a Concrete Tile Roof? – Kindle, Softcover/Paperback (https://a.co/d/06KU2AY9).

4. Faithful Finances: A 10-Day Biblical Jump Start to Financial Freedom – Kindle [Amazon] (https://a.co/d/08RZgcXU).

Final Thoughts

By following the guidance in this comprehensive book, you will be well-prepared to file and manage an investment property insurance claim effectively.

From understanding your policy to navigating the claims process and maximizing your settlement, each chapter provides practical insights and expert advice to help you protect and benefit from your property insurance.

Should you find any errors of any kind, please contact the author at sashorrosh52159@aspirewords.com.

We appreciate your purchase of these resources and wish you the absolute best toward living your very best life.

If you like the book and find it valuable, please consider giving us an honest Review on Amazon and sharing the link with others.

I thank you,

Sam Shorrosh, Ph.D.

www.ingramcontent.com/pod-product-compliance
Lightning Source LLC
Chambersburg PA
CBHW072051230526
45479CB00010B/664